50 THINGS TO KNOW BOOK SERIES REVIEWS FROM READERS

I recently downloaded a couple of books from this series to read over the weekend thinking I would read just one or two. However, I so loved the books that I read all the six books I had downloaded in one go and ended up downloading a few more today. Written by different authors, the books offer practical advice on how you can perform or achieve certain goals in life, which in this case is how to have a better life.

The information is simple to digest and learn from, and is incredibly useful. There are also resources listed at the end of the book that you can use to get more information.

50 Things To Know To Have A Better Life: Self-Improvement Made Easy! by Dannii Cohen

---

This book is very helpful and provides simple tips on how to improve your everyday life. I found it to be useful in improving my overall attitude.

50 Things to Know For Your Mindfulness & Meditation Journey by Nina Edmondso

---

Quick read with 50 short and easy tips for what to think about before starting to homeschool.

50 Things to Know About Getting Started with Homeschool by Amanda Walton

50 Things to Know

I really enjoyed the voice of the narrator, she speaks in a soothing tone. The book is a really great reminder of things we might have known we could do during stressful times, but forgot over the years.

- HarmonyHawaii

50 Things to Know to Manage Your Stress: Relieve The Pressure and Return The Joy To Your Life

by Diane Whitbeck

There is so much waste in our society today. Everyone should be forced to read this book. I know I am passing it on to my family.

50 Things to Know to Downsize Your Life: How To Downsize, Organize, And Get Back to Basics

by Lisa Rusczyk Ed. D.

Great book to get you motivated and understand why you may be losing motivation. Great for that person who wants to start getting healthy, or just for you when you need motivation while having an established workout routine.

50 Things To Know To Stick With A Workout: Motivational Tips To Start The New You Today

by Sarah Hughes

50 THINGS TO KNOW ABOUT BECOMING AN ENTREPRENEUR

Robert Ermeta

50 Things to Know

50 Things to Know About becoming an Entrepreneur Copyright © 2018 by CZYK Publishing LLC. All Rights Reserved.

All rights reserved. No part of this book may be reproduced in any form or by any electronic or mechanical means including information storage and retrieval systems, without permission in writing from the author. The only exception is by a reviewer, who may quote short excerpts in a review.

Cover Image: https://pixabay.com/en/business-documents-smartphone-3224643/

CZYK Publishing Since 2011.

50 Things to Know
Visit our website at www.50thingstoknow..com

Lock Haven, PA
All rights reserved.
ISBN: 9781723863073

50 THINGS TO KNOW ABOUT BECOMING AN ENTREPRENEUR

50 Things to Know

BOOK DESCRIPTION

Are you tired of working for someone else?

Do you have a dream product or concept that you think the world needs to know about?

Are you willing to put in the work, and the long hours, to make your dream succeed?

If you answered yes to any of these questions, then this book is for you.

50 Things to Know About Becoming an Entrepreneur by Robert Ermeta, offers an approach to the subject that many other books don't. Most books on Entrepreneurism tell you to that the challenges are worth the rewards that you will reap. Although there's nothing wrong with that, they never explain what those challenges are, nor what they will cost both financially and mentally. Based on experience, and a strong educational background, Robert takes the time to dive into topics that most Entrepreneurs don't like to discuss.

In these pages you'll discover exactly what is required to become an Entrepreneur. This book will help you decide if being an Entrepreneur is something that is right for you, and your success will be strictly determinate on the work you are willing to put in.

By the time you finish this book, you will know the pros, and cons, of becoming your own boss. So grab YOUR copy today. You'll be glad you did.

50 Things to Know

TABLE OF CONTENTS

50 Things to Know
Book Series
Reviews from Readers
BOOK DESCRIPTION
TABLE OF CONTENTS
DEDICATION
ABOUT THE AUTHOR
INTRODUCTION
WHAT TO KNOW
1. Be Your Own Boss
2. Read Books
3. Interview Entrepreneurs
4. Time Management
5. SMART Goals
6. Networking
7. Tradeshows
8. Elevator Pitch
9. Unplug and Unwind
10. Watch the Doubters
11. Be Prepared to Fail
12. If You Fail, Do It Fast
13. Long Hours
14. Being Broke
15. What's Your Why?

50 Things to Know

16. Self-Motivate
17. Set Goals and Stick to Them
18. Create A Routine
19. Know Your Numbers
20. Give to Get

MONEY & COSTUMERS

21. Cost of Hiring/Firing
22. Cost of Customer Acquisition
23. Not All Customers Are Right for You
24. Titles
25. Government Assistance

SOCIAL MEDIA

26. Facebook/Twitter
27. Instagram/Snapchat
28. Website/Email

PERSONALITY

29. Myers Briggs
30. Extraversion or Introversion
31. Sensing or Intuition
32. Thinking or Feeling
33. Judging or Perceiving
34. Customer Segments
35. Value Proposition
36. Channels
38. Revenue Streams
39. Key Resources

40. Key Activities
41. Key Partnerships
42. Cost Structure

BUSINESS PLAN

43. Mission Statement
44. Vision
45. Values
46. Positioning
47. SWOT Chart
49. Pricing Strategy
50. Executive Summary

50 Things to Know

DEDICATION

This book is dedicated to the educators whom I had the privilege of learning from during my time at Mohawk College.

Rob Belchior, who taught me the value of the customer.

Gord Bereza, who taught me to always know my numbers!

James Cowan, who taught me the importance of the perfect Business Plan; tedious, but necessary.

Laura Cole, who taught me the importance of personalities and behaviors, and what they can mean to a business!

Melanie Sodtka, who taught me to market, to network, and to have the perfect pitch prepared to use on the fly!

All your lessons have been so influential to who I have become as an entrepreneur, and as an individual.

50 Things to Know

ABOUT THE AUTHOR

Robert Ermeta, owner and baker of Confectionary Creations, currently lives in Hamilton, Ontario with his husband, Cody, and their three cats (yes, that is a lot of cats). He runs his bakery/catering business out of his apartment, with the help of any family willing to lend a hand. When he is not wrist deep in dough he works as a manager for a large Canadian based entertainment company.

Robert, having a passion for education, has a certificate in Architectural Technology, a bachelor's Degree in English and History, and an Honors Certificate in Small Business and Entrepreneurship. Having realized his dream of establishing his own business, he has ventured into the world of writing, in hopes of sparking others to make their dreams a reality.

With an honors certificate, and his own established business in Hamilton, Robert would like to share his story with others, by showing 50 things that he feels you need to know about becoming an Entrepreneur. The positive, and negative things, that need to be thought about before venturing into such a daring field.

50 Things to Know

INTRODUCTION

"All our dreams can come true, if we have the courage to pursue them."
~ Walt Disney

Be your own boss; it sounds cliché, but often this little statement is uttered around the world by those who are fed up with where they are at in their lives. Often times you hear various, self-defeating statements that keep these people exactly where they are. They are either too young or have no experience. Perhaps they feel like they have nothing worth selling or can't think of a product. Often times it is the older generation feeling like starting a new career would be too hard. If any of these statements sound like you…..snap out of it!

You are never too old to try something new; and by that logic, you are never too young either. If you are making up excuses then you are either comfortable where you are, or you are afraid of where you might end up. The comfort is not something that will be easy to shake, but the fear is something that you need. Embrace that fear as a friend, and let it be the driving force behind everything you do going forward. Once you realize that fear, it can no longer control you.

Being an Entrepreneur is one of the best careers out there, because you are at the helm of your greatest achievement yet! Of course, many people feel like they might not have a product that is worth selling, or nothing original. Do you think that matters? I have friends who have started up their own businesses in Landscaping, and Dancing. None of these are new ideas, but their business models and what they have done to this existing market is incredible! Sure there are many studios out there, and many companies that can mow your lawn, but these individuals have seen those companies, examined their weaknesses, and turned them into strengths of their own.

If you are wanting to be an Entrepreneur because you hate your job, and you want to do something that you believe gives you more meaning in life, then by all means give it a go! I do advise that you think this through, as the next steps (which can take years) can be rough, but if you're up for the challenge then read on!

WHAT TO KNOW

"Don't let others convince you that the idea is good when your gut tells you it's bad."

- Kevin Rose

1. BE YOUR OWN BOSS

Be your own boss. Majority of entrepreneurs start their journey with this as their jumping off idea. The thought of never having to meet deadlines, or complete projections, often entices younger minds into believing that entrepreneurism is the way to go. While being an entrepreneur does technically mean that you are your own boss, that doesn't mean you suddenly have no responsibilities.

Being your own boss is one of the hardest things going. You still have those deadlines to meet, and those projections to figure out, but you have no one holding you accountable. This is where most trouble as an entrepreneur can stem from. You start pushing those deadlines, until you have clients and investors breathing down your neck. You go from being your own boss, to having multiple bosses. Your clients demands suddenly push you back into a familiar place; you no longer have the control and freedom that you thought you would get from being in charge.

Perhaps one of the biggest things to remember is to stay on top of your duties. Set your deadlines, and fulfill your projections, but above all else stay on top of them! If you can manage to keep everything scheduled, and follow that schedule, then not only will you be your own boss, but you will be an effective one.

2. READ BOOKS

It may sound odd to hear this, especially when you are out of school, opening your own business, and have some experience under your belt. Books can help you out in many ways. By reading books from current entrepreneurs you can get a better perspective on exactly what you should expect during your journey.

There are many books out there that tackle the ins and outs of being an entrepreneur. If you look, you can find books written by authors who have created businesses in your field of interest. They may help you to understand things you didn't before or give you insight on things you hadn't even considered.

The books you read don't all have to deal with entrepreneurism, but a few of them should. You should ensure that you have all the knowledge you can about your field of interest before setting out. Grab books from entrepreneurs who have made it, and are extremely successful, but also grab books from entrepreneurs who crashed and burned. Both perspectives will be increasingly helpful to you along the road (and it's a long road, so you'll have plenty of time to read).

If you hit a book that mentions other authors to check out, do it! More books mean more knowledge on the subject at hand. Eventually you will hit a wall where you feel like you have answered all questions that you have, and even some you didn't know you had!

3. INTERVIEW ENTREPRENEURS

This may be one of the most helpful things that you will take from this book. Find entrepreneurs in your field of interest and ask them if they would be available for a meeting where you can ask questions. Some will not be okay with this, afraid that you may become a threat to their business, but many understand where you are coming from, and will help you as much as you can.

Go in with a professional attitude and appearance, and do not barge right in with questions. Start with some small talk, and get a conversation rolling. If you can get a decent momentum built up for a conversation, and then start asking some definitive questions, it will seem less like an interview and more like a casual meeting among business partners. This is what you are aiming for.

Keep in mind that if you are meeting with an entrepreneur who operates in the same field as you, you may be speaking with a future competitor; you could also be speaking with a future **Strategic Alliance** (more on that later).

4. TIME MANAGEMENT

Another important lesson that all entrepreneurs need to learn, and keep in mind, is the importance and value of time management. It sounds rather simple, and really it should be, however time management is one of the hardest things for an entrepreneur to grasp. When you first start out in your business you may find yourself acting as the manager, employee, and volunteer all at the same time. You will end up running yourself ragged trying to keep up with everything that is going on, and you will use the excuse that there just isn't enough time. That is where you are *almost* always wrong.

I implore you to give yourselves three days to complete an assignment that worked wonders for me in college, and really opened my eyes. Keep a notebook with you and keep a time log of the next 48 hours. Do not do anything differently then you would on a normal day, simply write down the times that you are completing certain items. For example, wake up 8am, bathroom until 8:05am, cooked breakfast and ate until 8:30am, etc. It does sound like a tedious task, and may seem odd, but I promise you the results will absolutely astound you!

The amount of times I used to utter "I just don't have enough time" amazed me, and this task enlightened me. As it would turn out I had all the time in the world, more then I actually knew what to do with. The issue was that I never used my time productively. If I had down time I would spend them lounging and watching TV, or scrolling through Pinterest, instead of doing something of value. I'm not saying you can never have down time but try to limit it until when your work is done. Do you commute to and from your business via public transit? Try and incorporate some productive activities in your commute, such as checking and responding to emails, or planning your day out. You will find that you have more time than you think, you simply don't use it correctly!

5. SMART GOALS

You will always hear people saying that you need to set goals for yourself when you're an entrepreneur, and that is true. You have no one to hold you accountable except for yourself, but the worst thing you can do is set goals that you have now way of reaching, or tracking. This is when SMART goals come into play. SMART goals are Specific, Measurable, Actionable, Relevant, and Time bound.

Specific goals are those that dive into a problem head on in the most specific way possible. A way to look at this is by considering the following three goals: Get healthy, lose weight, and lose ten pounds. While the first goal, get healthy, sounds like a great goal, it does not tackle a very specific target. Are you going to get healthy by eating better, by working out, by being more active? You need something with a little more specificity. The second goal is a little better, lose weight, but still isn't very specific. Do you plan on losing a certain amount of weight before you stop? Finally, the third goal, lose ten pounds, is specific. You have given yourself a target that has a clear finishing point; losing ten pounds.

Measurable means the goal needs to have a way to track its progress. In the example of losing ten pounds, you can easily measure this goal with a scale. You can see the scale moving towards your goal weight, giving you something that you can keep track of.

Actionable simply describes that work that is going to go into the goal. If the goal you have picked has too many actions to succeed, then you may want to consider breaking down your goal further. For the goal of losing ten pounds your actions may be to eat three meals a day, cut our snacks, and work out. This gives you three actionable procedures in which to help you achieve your goal.

Relevant is a way to monitor your goals and ensure that you are pursuing the correct goal at the time. You may want to place your goal on a chart showing the effort put in, and the value gained from the goal. If the value gained is worth less then the effort it is taking to complete the goal, then you may not to go after a different goal.

Finally, time-bound simply means to give yourself a deadline. If your goal is to lose ten pounds, then you can start right away and maybe lose ten pounds in twenty years. There is a chance that isn't the result you were looking for. Now if you give yourself a time-bound goal of losing ten pounds in six months, you have a clear deadline of when you want to complete the goal in mind.

6. NETWORKING

While this is important, it is often something that entrepreneurs don't think of as useful or consider it tedious. Networking is something that could make or break you as an entrepreneur. You will not grow a company by keeping it to yourself, and by relying on your webpage to bring you business. You need to be willing to go out, pound the pavement, and talk to people about what you have to offer. Find local networking events in your city, or surrounding cities, and start going to them. Bring business cards and some knowledge on your industry and be ready to talk to as many people as you possibly can.

Networking gives you a chance to discuss your business and hear from other entrepreneurs as well. If you haven't had a chance to interview entrepreneurs as mentioned before, then this is the perfect opportunity for you to ask as many questions as you possibly can. The thing to keep in minds is that everyone at a networking event is there for the same reason, so don't shy away. Be approachable, be courteous, and be sincere. Keep those three things in mind and you will thrive!

7. TRADESHOWS

As an entrepreneur you should constantly be trying to think of new ways in which to introduce your product/business to the world. The easiest way to hit a lot of people at once is to take part in a tradeshow (or a craft show depending on your product). For example, as a baker, my items tend to sell fairly well at any Christmas craft shows that I attend. The people there are all doing some browsing and stop by my booth for a quick snack. The secret is that I'm not there to sell my product at all.

The main reason to frequent these tradeshows is to get your name out there. You need to think of the cost of a booth as an investment in your business. If you can sell some of your products then obviously that's a bonus, but that shouldn't be the main reason why you're there. Make sure to have some sort of deal set up if you are selling your products. You want something that is going to at least get them to follow you on social media, so perhaps offer a 10% discount on anyone who proves that they have liked your page.

True, they will most likely forget that they have liked your page, but they will now see any posts that come up, reminding them of your business.

If you can convince a friend to come with you, and can trust them to run your booth for a little while, it is always a good idea to take a walk around the floor and visit the other booths. You are specifically looking for businesses that are selling the same kind of items as you. Take a look at what they are offering, and what they are doing to get customers to stick around and make purchases. Are they offering something that you don't currently offer? Are they giving larger discounts, or perhaps giving away free items? You now have inside knowledge as to what your competitors are willing to do to be the best in the field, and you need to be prepared to step up!

If you don't have the chance to purchase a booth or table at a tradeshow, you should at least make sure to visit them. A tradeshow doesn't necessarily have to be completely dedicated to your business for you to have interest. For example, as a baker I would love to visit tradeshows dealing with baking, however I would also visit catering tradeshows, wedding shows, even event shows. All of these are loosely related to my field and deserve my attention.

8. ELEVATOR PITCH

The elevator pitch is something that needs to be perfected if you want to succeed as an entrepreneur. If you have ever seen an episode of Dragon's Den, or Shark Tank, then you know exactly what a pitch is, and how vital it can be. If you haven't seen an episode of either, but this book down, watch a few seasons, and then come back to me. The entrepreneurs on those shows have a few minutes to pitch their product/business to the investors, and then discuss the financial aspects of the business. They have upwards of ten minutes, depending on the product, and can really dive into their company's back story. You may not ever be as lucky to have someone who is being paid by a production company to sit and watch you talk. This is where the elevator pitch comes in.

Think about the amount of time you spend on an elevator on average. Depending on the floor you are heading to, and the amount of stops in between, you are looking at 60 to 90 seconds. That is the amount of time it should take you to pitch your product to someone. Work in as much detail as you can, without overwhelming the listener, and try to leave out financials if you can. When in a meeting with an actual investor you will have time to discuss everything, but at networking events the elevator pitch can make all the difference in the world.

9. UNPLUG AND UNWIND

The last "chapter" of this section is perhaps the most important. It is important to your business because it is important to your health and wellbeing. You are an entrepreneur, meaning you have spent most of your waking day worried about your business, are working in it. You have taken every chance you could to grow that day, and you are now at home. This isn't the time to answer emails or plan your following day. This is your time to unwind.

I suggest leaving your laptop, phone, tablet, or any other device connecting you to your business in a separate room. Make it a habit to leave work at work. Sure, this goes for almost any profession, don't bring work home with you, but as an entrepreneur it can often be more difficult. You need a chance do debrief and relax before hitting the grindstone again the next day.

Plan a day or two during the week where you can afford to get away from the job as well. At first this may be a little difficult, but eventually you will have at least one employee working for you (depending on the business) that you can trust to handle things for 24 hours while you recharge. Take this time for family, for friends, or to binge watch the latest episodes of Shark Tank on Netflix!

WHAT TO WATCH OUT FOR

"You have to see failure as the beginning and the middle, but never entertain it as an end"

- Jessica Herrin

10. WATCH THE DOUBTERS

Something that all entrepreneurs will have to deal with at some time are the doubters. They can take many forms, but most often it is your friends and family that have they most doubts. As an entrepreneur you need to become proficient at shrugging these doubters off.

Your parents will often have the most concern for you. This isn't necessarily due to their lack of confidence in you, but rather a concern for you that they feel rivals your passion. They are concerned with how much it will cost to start up, how much effort it will take to get things going, and how much stress this might place on you as the owner and operator of your own company. You won't have the option of leaving things for someone else to take care of, so they will worry that you will become too run down from all the work required. You need to be able to sit down with them, calmly, and explain that you have already weighed out the pros and cons and you feel confident in your decision.

Your friends will often build you up, but that can change. At the beginning you will notice that they are supportive and have offered to help you out along the way. You accept their help and you start making your dreams a reality. A few weeks after your launch they invite you to a weekend at a cottage, which you decline because you simply do not have the time. They are understanding and let it go. A month later they invite you again, but again you must decline because business if booming and you must be there for your company. Eventually you start rejecting their plans involving you being gone for more than a few hours which upsets them. This is when their doubts will start rolling in. You need to be ready to sit down with them and explain your position.

11. BE PREPARED TO FAIL

This chapter is going to sound a little negative, but it's something that I was taught and has helped me immensely throughout my journey as an entrepreneur. The fact is that more than half of all small businesses crash and burn within their first 3 years. The fact is scary but it's something that entrepreneurs needs to understand. You might think that you have the best product in the world, something that everyone needs to have in their lives, but what proof do you have? Sure, your test audience loved it, but were they friends and family? Were they just trying to protect your feelings? You have now opened a business revolving around this self-proclaimed revolutionary product….and no one wants it. You've wasted your life savings in creating this business and you have managed to lose it all. I'm sorry to say that sometimes this happens.

Before you decide to go into business for yourself and launch your own product you need to have a few months (if not years) of trying out your idea and seeing if there is a market for it. I have had the fear of opening my own brick and mortar bakery and because of this I have created a home run business catering for weddings and small events. I could easily open a shop, and would probably have the customers to do so, but I don't have that confidence level yet. Until that confidence level hits I won't venture into owning my own store front. Eventually I will have to take the plunge, and I will be ready for it then. However, I could still fail and that is just a reality that I must face.

Take some time with your product and test it out on your desired market. If it is a physical item that you can sell then try renting some space in a fair, or at a tradeshow, and see if you can push your product there. Create pop-up shops around your city (if you legally can) and see how you do with those sales. These little fairs and shows may not bring you a huge revenue spike, but they will allow you to test running your business in a public setting and give you a chance to prove that you have what it takes.

12. IF YOU FAIL, DO IT FAST

Let's stick with this negative subject for a little while longer. Another lesson that all entrepreneurs must learn is that if you fail you need to accept it and fail fast. As an entrepreneur you have decided that your product is something everyone needs, and you were very wrong. You tell yourself that a little more advertising will help push the product, and perhaps new brands and packaging as well. You are then spending more money on a product that isn't making you any money to begin with. Before you know it, you are hemorrhaging money at an alarming rate. You have now slipped into the failure that most entrepreneurs face, and you could have avoided it all together.

At the first sign of failure you need to decide: is your product *actually* going to improve with a few minor tweaks, or is it a lost cause? If you can make some minor changes in the product and you notice a spike in sales, then ride that wave and see where it gets you. If you decide that the product is a lost cause, then you need to bail fast. The worst thing you can do is put more money into the product knowing that it may not help. That is why if you fail you need to fail fast. Realize your mistakes, disband your business, and get out. Take another year improving the product on your own time and try again when you have something you might sell. You need to know that failure is a possibility but shouldn't be the reason you stop trying.

13. LONG HOURS

Many entrepreneurs decide that they want to open their business because they have this idea in their mind that once the business is established they will be able to sit on a beach somewhere and reap the financial gains of said business. WRONG. In fact, what most entrepreneurs don't realize is that amount of work that will go in to owning and operating your own business. The idea of taking extended vacations should be the furthest thing from your mind.

A read a book in college that discussed a certain entrepreneur who opened her own pie shop. She was a talented baker, and her friends convinced her to open her own pie shop. Now, she wasn't able to afford any help at first, so she was the owner and operator of her business, like many of you will be. She found herself in her shop as early as 4am to start prepping the pies for the day. The shop opened at 9am and closed by 5pm. She then had to spend the time cleaning and tidying up and taking inventory for the next day. She would leave the shop by 7pm, go to the market to purchase ingredient for the next day, and be at home by 9pm. She would have a quick bite to eat before heading to bed, and then would repeat everything again the next day.

I am not suggesting that you will have as busy a day as this entrepreneur did, but you can (and should) expect to be working long hours. Being an entrepreneur comes with benefits that you can cash in on later in life. When you are established enough to have staff that can manage the building without you for a week or more then you will have time to step away, but until then you have a daily job that is very demanding and time consuming. You need to be okay with working long hours, having limited time off, and losing most of your social life. It's not easy, but it can be done.

14. BEING BROKE

This section is often the hardest section to read and hear about. You have decided to open your own business and be your own boss. You have a product or service that you think people just can't live without. You realize that you were right, and this product is high in demand. So high in demand that you need to order a large surplus of stock to get you through the month. Doing this takes most of the money in the company account, and you realize that you won't be getting paid this month. That's okay, you can take a cut next month.

Surprise! Next month you have the same issue, and the month after that as well. You start to realize that unless something changes this isn't going to be a business that you can start taking money from. A friend of mine opened his own coffee shop in our cities downtown core, and I would always ask him for advice while attending classes about entrepreneurism. When I asked him how it feels to have money he chuckled. For the first year of operation he had never actually taken a pay cut for himself. He had employees that needed to be paid, bills that needed to be paid, and loads that needed to be paid back. It wasn't until a year after opening that he was bringing in enough to take a modest amount off money here and there...not even a steady paycheque.

You need to keep in mind everything that is going to go into this business, and everything that is going to need to be paid. If it wasn't for my partner I don't think opening my own business would even be an option. In some cases, my friends for example, he worked a second job while operating his business. You may not have a choice. You still need to live and running a business where you are not profiting will not make living easy. You just need to hold out hope that it will all be worth it in the end.

#ENTREPRENEURLIFE

"Don't get distracted. Never tell yourself that you need to be the biggest brand in the whole world. Start by working on what you need at the present moment and then what you need to do tomorrow. So, set yourself manageable targets."
- Jas Bagniewski

15. WHAT'S YOUR WHY?

This is often another difficult area for entrepreneurs, mainly because they don't really know why they are attempting to do what they are doing. Sounds a little confusing doesn't it? You have this great idea for this amazing product that you think people need. You have spent time and money developing this product and getting it ready for sale, and then someone asks you "Why did you create it". You can't think of an answer except "because people need it".

The idea behind "what's your why" is specifically what's *your* why. Investors and customers don't want to hear that you created the product because people need it, they want to know why it struck you as something people needed.

Not to toot my own horn, but my bakery is a perfect example for this section. If I haven't already stated I own and operate my own catering business where I deal with, specifically, vegan baked goods. Why do I handle vegan products? I saw a need that other companies were trying to fill but failing at. Many people have taken up the vegan trend, voluntarily opting out of the consumption of any animal products or biproducts. A close friend of mine is also vegan, but she is not vegan by choice. Through months of stomach issues, and a series of tests, it was concluded that she has an allergy to various enzymes that are found in animal products and biproducts. She was forced into veganism without much warning and adapted quickly.

A bakery in our area sells strictly vegan baked goods, but the price tag is astounding. A single cupcake can run a customer upwards of $5. And that is where I found my "why". Why should someone who is being forced into a lifestyle be expected to pay almost triple the price for something as simple as a cupcake. I mean, think about it, no animals products or biproducts means no milk, eggs, or butter. So, what is in these cupcakes that make them so expensive? Nothing, except for the vegan title! Through research and trials, I created a vegan recipe that costs the same as a regular recipe. The result; vegan cupcakes at a generic price.

I am not expecting every entrepreneur to have a back story as similar or passionate as mine, but when asked why you created a product there must have been a reason close to you to do so, and you should be proud to share that reason with whoever asks!

16. SELF-MOTIVATE

As an entrepreneur you may find yourself falling into a bit of a rut when it comes to your business. You have opened shop, it has been a few weeks, but business isn't booming as much as you had anticipated. This rut can often cause entrepreneurs to start doubting themselves and being thinking about giving up. At this point you need to be able to motivate yourself to do more.

You may have friends who stop in and work with you, which will brighten your day, but when it comes down to it this is your business, and this is what you wanted to do. Don't rely on your friends to pick you up, rely on yourself. Motivate yourself with little rewards to make the business seem better. Don't look at a slow day as missed sales, but as gained time. Sure, you only had 10 customers come through your door, but that gave you time to work on the website and possibly gain more customers from online sales. You should never dwell on the negative, but always try to spin it into a positive. I know it sounds rather simplistic, but you need to keep your spirits up to succeed. A customer can tell when you've slumped, and that will often drive them away.

Motivate yourself to gain more customers, to think of new products that will bring people in, to create a few campaigns or promotions. Whatever it is you need to do, do it!

17. SET GOALS AND STICK TO THEM

Something that we have been taught since our early years is to set goals and to stick to them. This goes for entrepreneurs and can often be quite a saving grace. You need to be very organized as an entrepreneur, and you will have no one holding you accountable for failures or missed targets. You need to be able to set goals and targets and hold yourself accountable for them.

Perhaps you are noticing that you aren't having a lot of a certain product sell, and you've decided to make that your goal. By the end of the month you want to sell at least 50 of the slowest moving products. You set your goal, now it's time to follow through. Decide on ways that you can push this product. Do you have it hiding near the back of the store, is the price point too high, could you have your staff suggestive sell to push the product? Figure out what it is you can do to meet your goal and work towards it. If you reach your goal then that's great, and if you don't figure out why. They worst thing you can do is change your goal before you've ended the trial. When you change the goal, it is because you are often admitting defeat. Don't let that be an option. If you don't reach the goal you can investigate as to why and create a new goal (keeping in mind the reasons for the failure this time around).

18. CREATE A ROUTINE

Routines are important for lots of different professions, but as an entrepreneur they can be the reason you succeed or fail. By creating a routine, you are committing to the same actions rapidly, to achieve similar results day-by-day. Some people are great at creating a routine, others have issues sticking to them. You need to be able to create a routine and hold yourself accountable.

One issue most beginner entrepreneur have is working from home when they are in the process of creating a business. They know what they want to do, and what they need to do, butt they get distracted because they are at home. I had a professor who ran his own business from home and I asked how he was able to do it without any distractions or interruptions. He said that he had his own office set up in his house, and his family knew that from 9am until 4pm he was not to be disturbed while in said office. He would wake up at 8am, have breakfast, and then put on business clothing (suit and tie) and sit at his desk. Believe it or not this can help you out. Being in the attire can change your mind set. You are dressed for work, you are in your office, you aren't being disrupted, what a great routine to fall into.

Your routine can be anything you want it to be if it helps you be productive. The important thing to remember is that you need to stick to that routine each day. The minute you start switching up your routine is when things start to get missed, or you start convincing yourself that what you're skipping today won't be important tomorrow.

19. KNOW YOUR NUMBERS

I've already mentioned Shark Tank and Dragon's Den a lot previously, so why not mention it again? Have you watched an episode since the last time I asked? Go watch one now, I'll wait. If you watch those shows like I do you will notice that one of the things that entrepreneurs get hit with the most is their lack of knowledge when it comes to their numbers. This is something you need to extremely careful with.

When you are speaking with an investor they will be asking you about your predictions, your profit margins, what you think your business is worth (mainly established businesses), etc. While stating that you don't know any of your numbers would be rather embarrassing, what would be worse is spewing off numbers that make absolutely no sense to the investors, nor to what you've been pitching up until this point. The rule of thumb when pitching is to give rough figures, not exact numbers. You want to let the investors know what you made in a fiscal year, and what you predict to do in the following year (or months if you haven't been in operation long). The trick is understanding your target customers and being able to explain why you have predicted the sales that you have. The last thing you want is to be hit with questions about your numbers that you can't answer. You need to be able to defend yourself and back your claims.

As an entrepreneur you need to know your numbers, know how to get those figures, understand your predictions, and know your net worth, and back up your claims. If you know nothing else except these items, then you are in good shape.

20. GIVE TO GET

While it may sound counterproductive, it has been proven that as an entrepreneur you need to be willing to give your product away in the beginning. You don't necessarily need to give it away for free but perhaps at lower price point then you would normally sell at. If you can afford to give some of your product away for free, then that is even better. Let's take a look at my bakery for an example.

While I do not own a storefront, I do advertise on social media quite often, and will often time offer contests. For example, I will have aa contest going to get page likes on Facebook. The contest will run for one week, and the customer who can get me the most likes gets 1 dozen cupcakes free of charge. This gets everyone interested in promoting the page for you. If someone is looking for a donation to a local charity I offer 1 dozen free cupcakes as a raffle prize. Even Stag and Does are a way to gain customers. I am known to donate 4-6 dozen cupcakes to a Stag and Doe I will be at, with the agreement that I can place my cards out nearby.

Now sure, it doesn't seem like this is costing me much as it's my product that I am giving away. But in the above examples, altogether, that is $160 worth of free product I have given out. That's not even including the time it would take me to prep the products either. However, this has now gotten my name out there to everyone involved. In most cases the Stag and Doe I donate cupcakes too contact me later to create their wedding cake. The person who wins the raffle often saves the coupon for a party and orders a few extra dozen. The contest winner gets 1 dozen free cupcakes, but each like can turn around and get me 20 more likes on my next contest. You need to be willing to spend money to make money.

MONEY & COSTUMERS

"If you can offer a free tier that provides a lot of value, it will naturally help you product to spread much more rapidly."
- Melanie Perkins

21. COST OF HIRING/FIRING

One big issue that entrepreneurs face is often the decision to hire employees. The decision is reached when the entrepreneur finally reaches the goals they have wished to achieve and are ready to start distributing some of the work load, so they can reap the benefits of being their own boss. Often hiring an employee is where an entrepreneur can find most of their financial issues, so you need to be careful and be prepared.

The cost of hiring an employee varies from business to business, but it is easy to calculate. You need to figure out exactly what they need to know to work in the business successfully. This doesn't mean to teach them everything up front, but simply to teach them what they will need to know to do the tasks that you plan on delegating to them. Let's say that it is going to take you 15 hours to have the employee fully trained in what they need to know. You now have to set aside 15 hours over a period of, at minimum, three days. Which means you need to have someone available to help you out while you do the training. If you include yourself in this calculation you are paying 3 different wages for 15 hours of labor. This doesn't include the cost of the uniform, or the cost of any potential mistakes they make during their first few weeks. This is where an entrepreneur needs to be careful.

You need to be very careful and selective during your interview process. While it will cost nothing to fire a staff member you will be losing out on everything you put in to training them. You will then have to turn around and do it all over again for the next employee you hire. This is often what starts to bring a business down, and where they start seeing red in their margins. Interview carefully, train well, and ensure that you are keeping up employee morale. If you have happier employees you will have less of a turnover.

22. COST OF CUSTOMER ACQUISITION

The cost of customer acquisition is something else that entrepreneurs do not tend to think of. It seems like something you don't really need to worry about. I mean, a customer sees your store, walks in, makes a purchase, and that's it. However, you need to think about what it takes to get the customer in there, and what it will take to get them to come back.

You will be paying for some form of advertising at some point during your launch, which is what will eventually get your customers attention. They will see your store and realize "Hey, that's something that I have been looking everywhere for" and will come in to check out what you have to offer. The advertisement brought them in, but you now need to engage them and make a sale. You also need to do it in a way that doesn't scare them off and will keep them coming back. The best way to look at this, and the cost associated, is to use a coffee shop as an example.

You open your own coffee shop and you have a trickle of customers who come in to test out the new products that you have to offer. Perhaps you are offering a maple flavored coffee that your customers will not be able to find anywhere else. You are expecting this maple flavored coffee to be your big seller, but your customers are a little reluctant to try it and stick to the original cup of joe that they know and love. You notice a customer that comes in to your store and stares at the menu and asks for a recommendation. You know have your in with that customers. You decide to talk about the new maple coffee that you offer, and they are intrigued but hesitant. They mention that the live a few blocks away and that this new shop is close enough for them to visit every morning, meaning this is a customer that you could get a lot of business from. Offer them the maple coffee and tell them it's on the house, but they must come back if they enjoy it.

It sounds cliché, and a little cheesy, but it has been proven to work. You have given away a cup of coffee, which cost you some money, but you have now gained a customer's trust and loyalty. They show up the next day and perhaps this time they buy a coffee and you mention that you have maple scones to go with it and offer them a scone to go with their coffee. I am not saying that you will always need to give out free product, but you now have earned customer loyalty with someone who will become a regular in your store. Even if you are giving away a scone, they have now purchased a coffee each day this week!

The price of customer acquisition is something that not all small businesses can afford. It all depends on the products that you are offering, and the expense. If giving away some products is something you can handle, then I would highly advise it. The coffee costs you $1.50, but the customer loyalty could earn you so much more.

23. NOT ALL CUSTOMERS ARE RIGHT FOR YOU

This is sometimes that hardest section for an entrepreneur to read and comprehend but it is true nonetheless: not all customers are right for you.

You are going to deal with all kinds of customers throughout your time as an entrepreneur, and you need to be able to tell those whom you want as loyal customers from those who you don't. In the business I work in we get customers from all walks of life and the entitlement some of these customers have is astounding. You have some customers who are pleasant and polite, and others who can be rude or condescending. The thing to remember is that this is your business and as such you need to learn to take command of who comes into your store.

While operating your store front you have two customers come in. The first customer (Rob) comes in, offers you a smile, and stands and looks at the menu contemplating their order. The second (Cody) comes in on their phone, offers you a smile, and takes their place behind the first customers. Rob approaches you and starts to ask questions about a few of the items, which you are happy to answer, before glancing up at the menu again. In answering Rob, you notice that Cody has ended his phone call and is waiting to be served. You kindly ask Rob if he would mind if you helped the next customer out while he decides what he wants. Cody steps up and places his order and rolls his eyes at how long it is taking Rob to decide. He makes a comment under his breath "It's coffee, it's not that difficult", which Rob hears.

As the business owner it is your job to know which customers you want to keep around, and which ones you don't want back. In this case Cody has made a rude remark and has commented on the speed of service. Perhaps you finish serving him, and then offer Rob a complimentary coffee because of the rudeness of the other customer. You need to remember that Rob was kind, not on his phone, and had a conversation with you during his visit. He is a customer you want coming back. While Cody did make a purchase, he put your other sales at risk with his behavior, and for that you had to give away product to rectify his error. Some customers you want, and some you don't. It's up to you to decide what to do.

24. TITLES

Depending on the business that you walk into you may here customers referred to as different things. You can have customers, clients, or guests. Believe it or not what title you offer to the customer says a lot about the business and service that you are providing. Granted, one business can utilize multiple titles depending on the product or service being offered, but most usually stick to one. Let's look at each one and give some examples of places where the titles exist.

Let's start by looking at the title of client. A client sounds like a very important person, someone who deserves a lot of special attention and care. You might be thinking that all your customers deserve special attention, and you're not wrong, however the level of importance is heightened on someone you are referring to as a client. For example, a mortgage broker would consider their customers to be their clients. Yes, they deal with multiple people in a day, but they are offering a specialized service to the individual, and they need to know personal information about that customer to continue. A photographer, a designer, even a commissioned painter would consider their customers to be clients. A bakery would not really consider their customers clients, *unless* something individual is being purchased. For example, someone buying a birthday cake, or a graduation cake would be considered a customer, as those are fairly generic items that are being purchased. However, if someone came in to have you design their wedding cake, you know have yourself a client.

Guest and customer are two terms that can essentially mean the same thing, however they can really set your business apart. When you hear the term customer and guest you may notice that one sounds a little more special then the other. Certain businesses like to use the term "guest" when referring to their customers, because it shows a certain level of elegance and sophistication. A customer is someone coming in, making a purchase, and leaving; a guest is staying and invited back.

An easy way to look at this is to look at a Starbucks and a local coffee shop (Tim Horton's for example). Tim Hortons is based on speed of service. They have tables set up but most of their customers are coming in, getting what they need, and getting out. At Starbucks your name is taken with your order, and you are called out specifically to pick it up. They have oversized chairs, and it is generally a very relaxed setting. To Starbucks you are a guest and are treated like a guest.

The different titles can mean all the difference to your business. If you are a photographer treating your clients like guests, you might be okay, but treating them like customers would send them packing. Going to Starbucks and being rushed due to speed of service would have you forgo ever visiting again. The titles you use are as important as the products you sell.

25. GOVERNMENT ASSISTANCE

The title of this chapter says it all; Government Assistance. As an entrepreneur you are often going to need to look for help wherever you can find it. The first place you should look is your local governments business section. Many governments offer bursaries for small businesses, depending on what it is that you will be offering. Some offer larger grants, or smaller loans that can be repaid on a lower interest rate then a bank may offer you.

The second place you should visit is the business center of your local city hall. If nothing else, you will find assistance there with the process required for opening a business in your municipality. Some cities offer you small business grants, while others might not have any grants to give out. Some also have intel on certain areas of the city where you should be opening your business, known as Business Improvement Areas (BIA). These are areas of the city that you may not have thought about opening a business because the area isn't highly visited and might not be in an area that your target customers are located. However, they are BIA's because the city has begun working on developing these areas to make them more of an area people want to visit. The idea behind a BIA is to get small business to open shops and operate in these areas for a lower rent then other areas of the city. This establishes the area as a business hub and will bring in more potential businesses and tenants in the months and years following. As the housing begins to build up around you, you find yourself operating in a neighborhood that has the target customers you were looking for all along. It may take a little longer to get some traction, but if it's something that you can afford then you should go for it!

SOCIAL MEDIA
26. FACEBOOK/TWITTER

In the growing digital age social media is becoming more of an asset for small businesses. When you first start out, a Facebook page can be a great way to start promoting your business for free. It might take some time to start building a following but that is time that you can consider an investment in your businesses future. You have a following of people who will now be able to keep up with everything that is going on regarding your business. You will also have a list of people to invite to your grand opening!

Facebook is also great because of its marketing an ad campaigns that you can run via their Facebook Business page. You can have

your business showcased on Facebook, with a target that you get to set. Perhaps your business involves delivering products, so you set a large radius for the ad to spread across; or perhaps it is something only offered to those in your city. Either way Facebook Business has you covered. The best part is that you can target whoever you please, and you can set a spending limit so that you don't break the bank.

Twitter is a little less business related but can help you to get a following. So many people use Twitter in their day to day lives, or just to scroll through. If you start tweeting about your business eventually those tweets will spread. What's even better is that you can link your Twitter and Facebook accounts together so that they coexist with each other. This makes things even easier on you!

27. INSTAGRAM/SNAPCHAT

Instagram and Snapchat are two other social media applications that should be considered for anyone who is thinking about starting their own business. The only difference is that these two apps will only come in handy for those business where visual are a part of the selling technique. I wouldn't expect to see a car mechanic using Instagram to promote their business, but I would expect a baker to use it.

Instagram also has ads that can be bought and used, much like Facebook, which can come in handy when you are trying to promote your business on a wide scale. The app allows you to set up your client base, your target demographic, and allows you to target people who have followed certain people. It is almost like the Netflix section "Because you watched…." only if focuses on those you've followed.

Snapchat is a little more complicated. While it does not necessarily have ad space that you can utilize, it can help you keep in touch with your followers and make your interactions with them more personable. Snapchat will be a little more time consuming however, as you will need to ensure that your customers are all following you. With Facebook, Instagram, and Twitter your posts have a chance of reaching people from others sharing or from promoting them. With Snapchat, only those who follow you will see any of your posts. If you are going to use Snapchat for your business be prepared to put in some extra time and effort.

28. WEBSITE/EMAIL

One of the biggest mistakes new entrepreneurs make is often with their website and their email addresses. It sounds silly but it's true. Often, entrepreneurs who are starting out don't feel like paying for a web domain or for a personalized email address, because they are not overly confident with their product. This is when you start seeing domains shared through Wordpress or Freewebs, and email addresses ending in @gmail.com. It is rather unprofessional and is more of a setback then it seems.

You are going to spend time creating this website, and you will have everything attached to the email address that you have now associated with your business. You will have "temporary" business cards created with this email address and website printed on them. Once you begin launching your business you will then start to get clients who will be contacting you via this email address.

Flash forward a few months, when you finally have clients and are possibly thinking of opening a brick and mortar store front. You are now realizing that you need a more professional website and email address and you now have the spare money to create both. In doing this you have no severed ties with the old web address (which all your clients are used to) and your old email address, which was your main form of communication. Yes, you have a store now, but any of your clients whom you only dealt with online will now have no way of connecting with you.

When you decide that your business needs a website and an email address take the plunge and purchase a domain and personalized address. You can find decent rates for under $100 a year and will not have to go through the hassle of relocating everything later.

PERSONALITY
29. MYERS BRIGGS

In 1917 Katherine Cook Briggs had begun research into personalities, based off of Carl Jung's conceptual theory that humans experience the world by utilizing four main functions – sensation, intuition, thinking, and feeling. She had noticed that different people had different personalities, and that some traits where more observable than others. She also noticed that because of these personalities people reacted to different things in different ways. She spent a few years studying this differences and similarities and eventually furthered Jung's research by concluding that there were 16 variations of personality that could be observed.

The idea that people experience the world using the four functions Jung stated still held true to Brigg's research, however she concluded that a person could have a mix of traits. The traits can be broken into deductive traits (intuition/sensing, introversion/extroversion) and inductive traits (feeling/thinking, and perception.judging). A person can have 1 of 16 possible variations of these, and no single person is the same, with various percentages of each trait present in different subjects.

The Myers Briggs Type Indicator (MBTI) is an important tool for entrepreneurs to use, especially if they will be dealing with partners or hiring employees. The MBTI gives you a way to almost pre-interview your candidates before sitting down with them. You let them go through a series of questions and in the end, you get an accurate representation of their personality type, which can help you with your hiring decision, or help you in the training process. If you understand their personality type, then you can understand how they are comprehending everything in their day to day lives.

The next few chapters deal with each type of personality and ends with an activity that can be done to help each person realize the truth in their type. A fun activity for you to do as an entrepreneur is to test out your ability to read people by getting your friends to participate in the activities. You will be able to assign them a letter for each of the four sections based on their answers. Then have them complete the MBTI at www.humanmetrics.com/cgi-win/jtypes2.asp and see if you are right!

30. EXTRAVERSION OR INTROVERSION

The first set of traits that a person can be assigned is either Extraversion or Introversion. What is often shocking is that we believe we are a certain way, but it isn't until after taking the MBTI test that we know. You might think you are the most introverted person in the world, but the MBTI steps in and says that you are 65% extroverted, and you start to realize that they may be right.

The fact of the matter is that this personality type doesn't strictly focus on your comfort levels in social situations but dives deeper into the core of who you are. We all understand extraverts as those who stand out in a crowd, the life of the party if you will. Introverts, on the other hand are those who are more refined, and often hang around by themselves, or with a small group of friends. The chart below helps to showcase exactly why this is not always the case.

Extraverts (E)	Introverts (I)
Often outgoing, talkative (sometimes they don't know when to stop)	Often quiet and shy, great listeners
Act before thinking	Think before acting
They find energy in a crowd	They need to recharge with privacy
Good at communication, and leading	Tend to be seen as ignorant and unaware of what's going on (because of their quietness)

You may think that you are an extravert in every way, and then you realize that often being a crowd drains you, and you need to recharge in a secluded area. If you consider each point above as 25% of your personality (for this type specifically), then you see that you are 75% Extroversion, and 25% Introversion. You can be a mix of both, and most people are, but you tend to ignore the lower percentage until you can see and understand it.

Activity: You are tasked with creating a list of points that will help to promote a local college to new students thinking of enrolling. What would your selling features be?

Answers: Extraverts will tend to create a list of social activities such as parties, concerts, dances, and the bars and pubs in the area. Introverts will create a list that focuses on the academic side of the school such as class sizes, the library, the professors, and even the school grounds themselves.

31. SENSING OR INTUITION

The next personality type has less to do with your social comfort, and more to do with what catches your eye. In this personality type, you often find a happy mix of both but sometimes a person can sway one way or the other. Sensing and Intuition can be better described as your attention personality; what do you pay attention to?

For someone who falls more into the sensing category, they tend to be much more factual in their approach to things, while an intuitive person will be more prone to that gut feeling. The chart below explains this better.

Sensing (S)	Intuition (N)
Facts and details	Endless possibilities
They look at what is	Trust their gut

present	
Focus on *real* things	What *could* be
They like to use what they have learned	They enjoy the learning process
They want you to get to the point	They don't like one point, prefer multiple

Again, a person can fit into both types, but one will always tend to be more dominant.

Activity: Ask your group to try to sell a visit to a local theme park to a stranger by creating a list. What about that theme park would draw them in.

Answer: Those with the Intuitive trait will give you answer that deal with thrills, and speed, and lots of "imagine….". Those who have more of a Sensing trait will list how many rides they have, what the speeds are, specific characters, perhaps even the weather. One deals in fact, the other in possibilities.

32. THINKING OR FEELING

The traits of Thinking or Feeling deal more with how you process and handle information that is give to you. An interesting way to look at this is by imagining yourself as the Tin Man or the Scarecrow from The Wizard of Oz. That's not to say that one has no heart, and one has no brain, but rather that each one uses what they have, as opposed to what they don't. In the movie the Tin Man (without a heart) is much more of a thinker, considering the options laid before him before taking a chance on anything. In retrospect, the Scarecrow (without a brain) looks more at how each option makes him feel and uses that to help him out.

We are the exact same as these two characters in a way. Some of us follow our brains, while other follow their hearts. There is nothing wrong with either approach, but perhaps a certain approach is better suited for a certain situation. For example, in a company that is heavily focused on numbers (an accountant) it would be better to have someone employed who is more of a thinker. In a guest service industry (Starbucks), you might be better to have the feeler employed. The chart below explains better.

Thinking (T)	Feeling (F)
objective	subjective
critique	compliment
Need to be right	compassionate
Feel good when a job is done well	Feel good when needs are met
Present goals and	Present points of

objectives first	agreement first
Brief and concise	Sociable and friendly

This personality looks closer at how you make your decisions, and whether you use your emotions to help you.

Activity: A friend shows up to a party wearing an outfit that you think looks horrible. Nothing matches, nothing is in style, and nothing fits right. What do you say to them?

Answer: A thinker will often start listing things that aren't right with the outfit, a feeler will find something good about the outfit and start with a compliment. The thinker will explain that the outfit is bad, and what needs to be change. The feeler will help the friend "fix" their outfit to make it work.

33. JUDGING OR PERCEIVING

The final personality type is one of my favorites to examine, because even though you might fit one profile, the other sneaks in somewhere. The Judger or the Perceiver looks more closely at what your world is like. For some this can feel like a breach of privacy (I'm looking at you Introverts), but for others you throw your doors open and say, "come on in I have nothing to hide" (hello Extroverts).

When thinking about this personality it helps to think about your bedroom closet. Did you cringe when I mentioned it? If so, then you probably fit into the Perceiving category. Did you have a sudden sense of pride? That fits you in with the Judging category. The main difference between the Judging and Perceiving crowds is mainly structural. The chart below explains this better.

Perceiving (P)	Judging (J)
adaptive	control
flexible	settled
spontaneous	closure
Likes options and freedom	Decisive, organized
Enjoys flexibility in their work	Plans their work
Adapts well to change	Likes structure and schedules

If you picture a desk, where your work will be done, then it is easy to see each personality. Those who are Perceivers will have a messy desk, with papers everywhere, and almost nothing in any order. They have deadlines to meet, but are often leaving everything until the last minute, and may need to be reminded. It may seem highly unorganized to you, but to them this is the perfect setting. You may not see organization, but often they know exactly where everything is.

On the other hand, the Judger would have a completely organized desk, complete with pen holder and sticky notes. They will tab their binders to make things easier to find, and they will have everything scheduled so they have time to complete everything. They might even get excited if the Perceiver asks for some help, because they can start to make sense of that bombshell of a desk.

The interesting thing here is that a Judger may also procrastinate and leave things until the last minutes. The Perceiver is doing this because they have either forgotten about the task, or they have run out of time. The Judger has planned for this procrastination. They knew that the task could be done last minute and left it until then.

Activity: Have the group write out a list for a party that they would like to go to. Tell them to include anything on the list that they feel is necessary.

Answer: The Perceivers will have included things such as BYOB, DJ name, dancing, games, bonfire, etc. They will be vague with the start time (when you get there), and the end time (before the sun comes up). The Judger will have everything laid out in an itinerary, with the exact time that each event will be happening over the course of the evening.

BUSINESS MODEL CANVAS

34. CUSTOMER SEGMENTS

The Business Model Canvas (BMC) is one of two tools that every entrepreneur needs to have ready for meetings, proposals, and investors alike. The BMC organizes each target market into 9 categories. For every target market that you plan on focusing on there should be a separate BMC created.

The first section of the BMC is the Customer Segments which is where you are going to outline what segment your target market fits into. There are 5 different types of customer segments are: mass market, niche market, segmented, diversity, and multi-sided platform.

The mass market is for businesses that have specific segmentation required. Their product is something that everyone needs and cannot live without. Perhaps they have niche products that they offer, but for the most part there is absolutely no segregation between customers. An example of this is a car; everyone needs to get around, and cars are generally what people use to do so. The niche market takes into consideration the needs of its target market. If we stick to the example of a car, the niche market would be a BMW or sportscar. While all customers in a mass market may be needing a car, only those in the niche market would think about purchasing such an expensive product.

The segmented market tends to narrow things down a little bit. A company will add additional segments, such as age, gender, or income, to their existing customer segment. The diversity market is made for companies who have multiple customer segments, all of whom have different needs and characteristics. A coffee company, such as Starbucks, could fit this market. While they serve coffee and beverages to the public, each person coming in tends to have a different need (highly caffeinated, caffeine-free, etc.). Finally, the multi-sided platform is made for businesses and companies that deal with multiple business platforms under their company names. For example, a credit card company will be able to help out their clients but will also offer assistance to the merchants who accept those credit cards. In this sense they are two separate markets.

35. VALUE PROPOSITION

The Value Proposition is where you want to position yourself as the best in the market for your own reasons. These tend to fall into either the qualitative or quantitative categories. The qualitative deals with customer satisfaction and outcome, while the quantitative deals with price and efficiency.

Most entrepreneurs get so caught up in their amazing ideas that they tend to fail when it comes to defining their value proposition. The easiest way to battle this is to set yourself up three columns: Products, Pain Relievers, and Gain Creators. You then need to think about the product that you are trying to push and start filing out these sections. Let's use Uber as an example.

By utilizing these three columns we can reduce them to create a meaningful value proposition. Their value propositions states that:

"Uber is the smartest way to get around. One tap and a car comes directly to you. Your driver knows exactly where to go. And payment is completely cashless"

36. CHANNELS

Channels are the ways that you deliver your value proposition to the targeted customers. Your channels will often be as unique as unique as your customer segments. You need to figure out a way to reach your target customers specifically. If you have created an effective channel it will something that is fast, efficient, and cost-effective. Channels can be anything from store fronts to major distributors. As an entrepreneur you need to figure out how your product is going to get to the customer it is meant for in the quickest way possible.

There are five types of channel phases that need to be considered during the entire process: awareness, evaluation, purchase, delivery, and after-sales. The first phase focuses on how you will start to make your product known. Will you use advertisements, social media, or word of mouth? Once you have figured out a way in which to present your product, you can move on to the second phase. In the evaluation phase you are creating a channel that your customers can use to review your products. Perhaps you will have surveys or set up online reviews. Either way you need to have this in place, as it tends to drive more customers to your products when they know others have used it and have had opinions about it.

The third phase is where you focus on the purchase aspect of your business. Are you a business that is going to have a brick and mortar store front, or are you more interested in the ecommerce side of things? If you are having an actual shop will you have cashiers or are you going to focus your business through self-checkouts? You then begin to get into the delivery side of things. Perhaps your product is something that can be simply purchased in store, which means the delivery portion is complete. However, you may have a product that needs to be delivered which means you need to know which company you will use, and whether that is the most cost-effective way for you to deliver that product.

Finally, you will dive into the after-sales phase, which focuses on everything that needs to happen for the customers after the sale of the product is complete. Is the product something that can be returned, or something that customers will require assistance with? Perhaps you offer tech support for your product, in which case a call center is needed. All these phases fit in to the channels section of your BMC and need to be thought of carefully.

37. Customer Relationships

The Customer Relationship portion of your BMC is the type of relationship that you will have with your customer segments. There are various forms of Customer Relationships that you can build, including personal assistance, dedicated personal assistance, self-service, automated service, communities, and co-creations.

The personal assistance relationship is often provided while the customer is in the process of purchasing the product. This represents the relationship between the customer and the employee during the entire sales process. This type of relationship often ends when the customer leaves the store with their purchase. To take this a step further you also have the dedicated personal assistance relationship, which offers much more of a hands-on approach to the service you provide the customer. If you think of the personal assistance as someone in a grocery store helping you find the right type of salsa, then the dedicated personal assistance is what you would receive when you go to purchase a vehicle.

The self-service relationship is where most companies are heading in todays industries, with the customers serving themselves. While some may argue that this is cutting jobs, and decreasing value to a business, many customers prefer to do things themselves. In a way you are empowering your customers to solve their own issues utilizing the tools you have provided for them.

The automated service relationship is something that businesses use to sell more products by getting to know the customer. It is very similar to the self-service relationship but has a more personalized aspect to it. Amazon is a great example of the automated service relationship. Customers are visiting the website in hopes of purchasing some last-minute Christmas items that they need without having to deal with employees or large crowds. While on the website they notice that Amazon has suggested a few extra items based on the ones they have already purchased. This is the automated service relationship taking over.

The community's relationship is a way for businesses to pair up their customers in a way that they can help each other out. We have all, at one time or another, found ourselves searching for a fix to something digital in our lives, and ended up on a community page. The page has many different customers posting about issues that they are having with the products, and then other customers explaining what they did to fix the issue. In most cases you find your answer and can fix the issue. In some cases, a representative of the company will also be live in the community to help answer any further questions you may have.

The final relationship is sometimes the rarest, which is the co-creation relationship. In this type of relationship, the company and the customer create a personal relationship through the customers direct input into the final outcome of the company's product or service. This can be seen in many different businesses, but lately many computer companies are working with their customers to create hybrid computers that do what the customer is expecting, with flares of colors and lights for a more personalized computer.

38. REVENUE STREAMS

The Revenue Streams is how a company makes their money off each customer segment that they have identified. While this does seem straight forward, there are actually different types of revenue streams to think about. You have asset sales, usage fees, subscription fees, lending/leasing/renting, licensing, brokerage fees, and advertising.

While businesses will not necessarily have all of these revenue streams present, a business can always have more than one. Some examples include

Facebook, Apple Music, and Netflix. While Facebook is a free webservice that can be used, they have a variety of games that are offered. These games are often free to play but have some in-app purchases that can be made to make the game better. In this case you have a usage fee tied in with your "free" website. If you take advantage of their advertising, then you are looking at yet another fee.

Apple Music is very much the same. You pay a monthly subscription fee in order to have access to unlimited music. However, the music comes and goes and sometimes you cannot find the same album again months later because it has been removed. You can always purchase a digital copy of the album by paying a fee, but that goes against the subscription fee you have already paid. This allows Apple Music to make some extra revenue.

Netflix does not have any "hidden" fees, nor do they offer in-app purchases...yet. You simply pay a subscription fee every month and enjoy access to whatever is streaming through Netflix for that month. When the month is up, and the programs shuffle, you have access to another set of programs for the same monthly fee.

When you are starting up your business you need to think about the revenue streams that you need to have, and those that you want to have. If you are a brick and mortar shop you will have asset sales of your physical items, but are you offering a subscription program for something as well? Will customers get a discount on items if they have a subscription already? You need to keep these questions in mind. Customers don't mind spending some money, but you need to make it worth their purchase.

39. KEY RESOURCES

This section of the BMC is self-explanatory. The key resources are those that are necessary to create any type of value for the customers that you have outlines in your customer segments. These items are assets to your company, as they are needed to keep the business going. These resources can be physical, intellectual, human, and financial.

Physical resources are your tangible assets that you need to make your company flourish. These items can range from equipment needed to create your product, to space you need to store your product. The Escape room craze that has hit the public would have "buildings" listed as one of their key resources. They need the space to conduct their business. As their business grows they will need to get more space to create more puzzles along the way. A bakery would need to have ovens, and mixers, and prep tables to have a successful business.

Intellectual resources are non-physical resources and can often include things like brands, patents, and copyrights. Your business can easily operate without any of these items (for the most part) but having them often offers you a type of security that you will need in the future. Perhaps you have created the newest craze and people are loving it! You would want to protect this with a patent and possibly even copyright it. This protects your business and creates a way for you to monetize the product. If I had created the first escape room, I would have patented the idea. I would then sell the concept to anyone who wanted to create their own. This keeps me as the leader of the craze, but also offers me another revenue stream.

Human resources are often the most important part of any business. This accounts for your employees, your delivery people, even your customers in some cases. Many companies thrive on the human resources component, making sure that their employees are will trained, knowledgeable, and friendly. Often these people are the faces of your company and can make or break a sale. You want to make sure that you have the right people for the job, and make sure that they stay happy with their work.

Financial resources tie together anything that fits into a financial category. This could include cash needed, and lines of credit. Some companies also offer the option for employees to purchase a stock in the company, which is another form of financial resource. You need capital to invest, and some start up cash to make your initial inventory purchases, which are all incorporated into this resource channel.

40. KEY ACTIVITIES

The key activities section of your BMC is the section where you are going to list off an explain what will be required of the company to deliver upon their value proposition. The mistake most entrepreneurs make with this section is assuming that their Key activity will be selling the product. While that will be an activity that will come eventually you need to think of everything from start to finish.

The first key activity that you should be thinking about is research and development. You have come up with a brilliant product that you think the world needs to see. You have spent a lot of time thinking about who the product will help, but have you done your research. At this stage you need to be willing to spend as much time researching what your product will achieve and developing it further so that there are no hiccups in the production stage. Many entrepreneurs hate the research portion because they just want to see their product completed and being used by the public. Why create a product that you are going to need to tweak the minute you launch it?

The second key activity you should place focus on is the production stage. This is the stage you need to use to put all your research and development ideas together. The product that comes from this stage should be something that needs no changes and is ready for mass production (when you are ready for that stage). This stage will then lead into the next stage which is marketing.

You have done your research, and you have developed and produced an amazing product that everyone needs. Now you must figure out how you are going to tell people about this amazing product. Again, more research is required here. The type of marketing and advertising that you do will be dependent on the customers segments you have created. For example, if your revolutionary product is something that only seniors would use you wouldn't want to put a lot of marketing effort into online campaigns. You may want to stick with radio commercials and even television commercials. However, for a younger customer segment, radio ads may not work but social media ads would. Do not fall into the falsehood that your research is done once the product is developed. Your research process should be ongoing.

The final stage, and possibly your final key activity, will be sales and customer service. You have marketed your product, figured out any issues that needed to be fixed, and you have now put it out to the public for sale. This is when you need to be on your A game. You need to be able to deal with the customers that you have coming in and be willing to do what it takes to make that sale. That could mean putting in longer hours, opening the store on days you planed on having it closed, and even forgoing on that vacation you had planned. You have a great product, but without customers you have nothing.

41. KEY PARTNERSHIPS

As an entrepreneur sometimes that best thing to have is a partnership with a like-minded individual or a company with similar products. For key partnerships we aren't talking about opening a business with a friend or business partner, but rather conducting your business in conjunction with another business for mutual gain. Partnerships can be a difficult thing to discuss because they involve a lot of contract and negotiations to ensure that both partners will be safe and secure during the linking of their businesses.

Generally, a business will take on a key partner to optimize their sales and improve their economy of scale; more ground to cover means more sales to make. They may also take on a partner to reduce any risks that may come from decisions they make. For example, perhaps two companies decide that they want to start selling a new product that they need to buy in bulk. The companies would split the bill and split the products. If the products don't sell both companies only see a 50% hit as opposed to working alone.

Key partners and partnership can be separated into four types: strategic alliances, co-opetition, joint-ventures, and buyer-supplier relationships.

A strategic alliance is a partnership that is formed between two non-competitors. They form a partnership because each business is successful in its own way, but each business can help the other. If you created a product that would be great to sell worldwide, but you only sell in Canada, you would want to find a strategic alliance with someone who has sales channels around the world.

A co-opetition partnership is when both partners are interested in something and agree to work together to share the risks that are associated. Perhaps two companies need a rare ingredient to complete their product, but it's hard to come by. It is within the interest of both partners to work together to collect this ingredient and assume the risks equally.

A joint-venture partnership is when two partners come together to create a new business. Each partner has expertise with their own business, but they feel like creating a new business, separate from their own, would be beneficial. A company that is known for brewing amazing craft beers may decide to go into a joint-venture partnership with an executive chef who owns their own restaurant. Together they create a new business where the beer is brewed on site, and the food is made in house. They each own and operate their own businesses still but have found a way to work together to create a new business.

The final partnership is the buyer-supplier partnership. This partnership is self-explanatory. This type of relationship could exist between local restaurants and local vineyards. The vineyard provides the wine to the restaurant who will turn around and sell it in their own business.

42. COST STRUCTURE

The final section of your BMC is the cost structure and might be the more important section of all. 90% of all small businesses fail within their first 3 years because the fail to consider the costs associated with everything they promised in their value proposition. When thinking about your cost structure you need to think about every cost that you will be incurring while operating your business. This can include everything from the rent required to operate a storefront to the fees required to run your website.

Your business will fall into one of two cost categories: cost-driven and values-driven. A cost-driven business is one that focuses on reducing the cost of a product; that is their value proposition. These businesses are more common than you would think and include things such as no-name grocery stores, no-name airlines, and even some no-name phone companies. These companies can offer you the same products as their counterparts but without the brand name backing them they can offer the services or products for a cheaper rate.

A value-driven business is on that forgoes looking at reducing cost and focuses on improving the value that they give to their customers. The product or experience itself may be pricy by the customers are accustomed to this type of service and will pay the extra for the service they receive. This can include hotels that predict your needs and provide for them, movie theatres that offer prime seating for an increased rate, or even Starbucks as opposed to a cheaper brand of coffee. Customers are willing to pay the extra cost to receive the increase in value of the services rendered.

BUSINESS PLAN
43. MISSION STATEMENT

When writing your business plan, you need to make sure that everything is in order, everything is clear, and nothing can be contested. In other words, do your research! There are two reasons for writing a business plan: you are a start-up business in need of funds to get things going, or you are an established business perhaps looking to open another location. For the remaining chapters we are creating a business plan for a start-up company.

Your mission statement is one of the first parts of your business plan and needs to be able to capture the attention of the reader. The idea is to create a short statement that identifies the purpose of the business and the goals of its operations. You can talk about the products or services that will be provided, the customers you want to reach, or even the area that the business will operate. They idea is to create a statement that draws in attention and makes the reader wonder "how"?

The best way to explain mission statements is to see some in action:

Cineplex – "Passionately Delivering an Exception Experience"

Starbucks – "Our mission: to inspire and nurture the human spirit – one person, one cup and one neighborhood at a time"

Amazon – "Our vision is to be earth's most customer-centric company; to build a place where people can come to find and discover anything they might want to buy online"

Google – "Our mission is to organize the world's information and make it universally accessible and useful"

44. VISION

Your vision, or vision statement, will follow your mission statement and should be an extension of your mission. You might have mentioned things in your mission statement that you can then provide further explanation on in your vision. Again, you don't want to go overboard, but you want to give some detail into what the vision of your business is.

Your vision can discuss the area in which the business will operate, and perhaps discuss being the only business of your type in the area. You can discuss the various steps you are going to take to ensure customer satisfaction and explain why you would do this. Again, seeing a vision statement is the best way to understand what I mean. The passage below is an excerpt from my own vision statement:

"...will focus on creating, and maintaining, long lasting relationships with both guests and suppliers, in hopes of becoming their go-to place for....will provide guests with the comfort of knowing their Vegan products are made in a separate area of the kitchen, with the same care and compassion that all their [items] are created with.....will be a company owned structure in Stoney Creek with approximately 2,200 square feet, allowing a seating capacity of 20 guests....will be very relaxed and can include...and an inviting office to meet with potential event coordinators"

You don't want to go into too much detail, but you do want to briefly outline what your company or business is going to do to follow the mission statement.

45. VALUES

Your values statement is what will follow the vision statement and should include the core values that your business will portray in order to achieve success. When creating your values statement, you need to be careful as to what you include, and you need to have proof to back up any claims.

Your statement can include things such as ethics, guests, service standards, environment, and even community involvement. However, as previously stated, be sure to back up your claims.

If you state that the environment will be taken into consideration as one of your values, you need to explain what you mean by this. For example, my business uses the Environment as one of their core values and states "...will run environmental awareness initiatives to ensure that they are keeping a small eco-footprint...all products that are not sold will be donated to local shelters, and majority of waste will be bio-degradable". This is a nice claim to make, but you need to have proof to back these claims up. This could include discussing with your local shelters as to whether they will accept these donations or having samples of the bio-degradable products that you mentioned.

The worst thing you can do in your values section is make a claim about a value and have nothing to back it up.

46. POSITIONING

The final section for your statements is your positioning statement. Your positioning statement is a way of explaining how your product or service will fill the customers need in a way that your competitors can't. While you don't want to necessarily call out your competitors you need to consider what it is that you do better. Perhaps you offer better rates, or you offer a better environment to enjoy your product. These are things that can be mentioned in your positioning statement. This statement "positions" you against your competitors and allows your investors to see what you will do differently than your competitors.

Another example from my own business plan:

"…is the go-to bakery for delicious, high quality, baked goods, both regular and vegan, for a guaranteed low price. The customer satisfaction rate is high, with many returning guests, looking for their fix of delicious [products] and Vegan treats, in a warm, inviting environment."

Looking at this example I have explained what it is I am offering, how the environment is in my store front, and why my business will beat out the competition; guaranteed low prices. I have positioned myself against other bakeries in the area, and in doing so I have put myself into my own market category that investors will take note of.

47. SWOT CHART

Just when you thought you were done researching, it hits you again! The SWOT Chart, or SWOT analysis is something that can actually be rather run as an entrepreneur (or stressful depending on how you look at it). SWOT stands for Strengths, Weaknesses, Opportunities, and Threats. As an entrepreneur you need to understand how your competitors work and operate. The easiest way to do this is to list your competitors in a chart and describe their strength, weaknesses, opportunities, and threats. And example of a SWOT Chart is below for bakeries.

The final row is meant to be reserved for your business, like the one above. Much like your competition you need to research your own business and be able to be critical. You may believe that you have everything figured out, but you will have some strengths *and* weaknesses and you need to be prepared to showcase them. Having a weakness isn't a bad thing, it just means that you understand where you may need to put in some extra work. That is why a SWOT chart can be a wonderful tool to use.

48. Financial Plan

The financial plan is going to be the meat and potatoes of your business plan. Everything leading up to this point has been describing your business and everything this it is going to offer. You were given a chance to show your passion for your business and describe just how you plan to see everything come to fruition. Now you need to explain the financials behind your plans. This is often one of the most difficult task for an entrepreneur because they have no idea what needs to be considered when thinking about the financials.

Often you will simply start to focus on the cost required to operate your business. Perhaps you will need a few thousand dollars to purchase the stock required to start everything up. That's a great start, but how did you get the storefront? Will you need a loan to open a shop, and if so how much will you need? Are you going to need equipment, or have you found a cheaper place to get the equipment that you need?

You need to consider everything when you are creating a financial plan. You will need to list any assets that you will have heading in, and any liabilities that you will incur during the process. You need to consider the cost of staffing your building, and whether they are hourly or salaried staff. You need to think about benefit packages, how much they cost, and how much you will contribute to them for each employee. When you start to work on the financial portion of your business plan, which should be the last thing you do before the executive summary, make sure that you have enough time to do as much research as you possibly can.

49. PRICING STRATEGY

The pricing strategy, in conjunction with the financial plan, is slightly easier to figure out. The pricing strategy comes into play when you are trying to compare your company to competitors and why your pricing is better. Not all business plans will necessarily have a pricing strategy, especially if they are more value-driven business, but the cost-driven businesses should have a pricing strategy ready to go. While you aren't going to call your competitors specifically, you are going to mention what you are doing to differentiate yourself from them. The example below is the pricing strategy I used for my own business:

…will offer delicious, always vegan, baked goods for the general cost of a "regular" baked good

from any of our competitors. The pricing will

start as low as roughly [price] per [product] to begin but will gradually increase until our competitors pricing is matched. There will be a savings built in to larger purchases, making it better to purchase a larger quantity. This ensures the product is moving and the guests are coming in.

All [product] will also follow the always vegan rule, however the cost point of each [product] will solely depend on the type of [product], and the style required. For simple frosted [product], with limited embellishments, the cost will be [price]. This cost will go up depending on flavor, embellishments, and occasions. There will be a higher cost on a [product] as there is much more time and planning involved.

The idea is to point out what you will being doing to match your competitors, or to increase your sales, from a pricing point of view. This isn't a place to discuss the environment, or the products offer, but rather what you will do to ensure that the best value is met for what is being offered.

50. EXECUTIVE SUMMARY

The Executive Summary will be the first part in your business plan, following your table of contents. The reason I chose to write about this part last is because it will be the last part that you write when creating your business plan. This summary is to give a brief 1-2-page summary of the entire business plan. An investor will take the time to look over your business plan *only* if they are intrigued by what your executive summary has to offer.

The executive summary must be well written, clear and to the point. It is the most important part of any business plan. As a start-up business your main goal for creating a business plan is often to convince an investor or a bank to lend you the money to start-up your business. Your executive summary should be sure to cover: the business opportunity, the target market, the business model, the marketing and sales strategies, the competition, the financial analysis, the owners/staff, and the implementation plan. While this book doesn't cover most of these items, they are easy to figure out once you have completed your business plan.

Be sure to keep your executive summary brief and to the point. If you start to put too much information in the summary the reader will begin to skim and may miss something. If they do not like what is written in the summary they will toss your plan to the side and begin reading the next one. The executive summary could make or break your start-up so be sure to follow the three rules mentioned above: clear, concise, informative.

READ OTHER 50 THINGS TO KNOW BOOKS

50 Things to Know to Get Things Done Fast: Easy Tips for Success

50 Things to Know About Going Green: Simple Changes to Start Today

50 Things to Know to Live a Happy Life Series

50 Things to Know to Organize Your Life: A Quick Start Guide to Declutter, Organize, and Live Simply

50 Things to Know About Being a Minimalist: Downsize, Organize, and Live Your Life

50 Things to Know About Speed Cleaning: How to Tidy Your Home in Minutes

50 Things to Know About Choosing the Right Path in Life

50 Things to Know to Get Rid of Clutter in Your Life: Evaluate, Purge, and Enjoy Living

50 Things to Know About Journal Writing: Exploring Your Innermost Thoughts & Feelings

50 Things to Know

50 Things to Know

Website: 50thingstoknow.com

Facebook: facebook.com/50thingstoknow

Pinterest: pinterest.com/lbrennec

YouTube: youtube.com/user/50ThingsToKnow

Twitter: twitter.com/50ttk

Mailing List: Join the 50 Things to Know Mailing List to Learn About New Releases

50 Things to Know

50 Things to Know

Please leave your honest review of this book on Amazon and Goodreads. We appreciate your positive and constructive feedback. Thank you.

50 Things to Know

www.ingramcontent.com/pod-product-compliance
Lightning Source LLC
Chambersburg PA
CBHW031438210526
45464CB00005B/2255